U.N.I

ROB CHILDS

ILLUSTRATED BY ANDY WARRINGTON

Ginn

CHAPTER 1 SUNDAY MORNING

I've never been lucky.

You might think that's a strange thing for someone to say, especially someone with a name like mine, but it's a fact. I really am very UNlucky!

You'll see what I mean as ... hang on a minute. You'll have to wait – we could be in here. Our winger's got the ball ...

"Yes, Jag!" I yell. "Give it to me!"

He passes it to me ... I can't miss!

"Shoot!" bellows Coach.

So I do, and ...

"GOAL!" I cry, just before my world turns upside-down. It feels like a tank has come crunching into me. I'm left flat-out, staring up at the sky. Talk about a late tackle. Any later and it would have needed a note to explain its absence!

By the time I manage to pick myself up and count all the pieces, the ball's back in our own half of the pitch.

"Are you okay, Lucky?" asks Jag.

"I think so," I say shakily. "What happened?"

"You hit the post."

"And what hit me?"

"Their big number five. He's a nutter."

"I heard that," snarls the giant defender, striding towards Jag. "I'll kick you right over that crossbar."

I'll say one thing for Jag – he's quick. But even I've never seen him move so fast!

Coach doesn't even seem to notice. Now he's stopped moaning at the referee, he turns his anger onto me.

"Why didn't you score?" he shouts across the pitch. He doesn't seem bothered that I've nearly had my legs chopped off at the knees.

"Don't worry. I'm fine thanks, Coach," I reply, knowing the sarcasm in my voice is wasted at that distance. So I give him one of my special stares as well. Coach knows all about my stares. Well, he is my dad too.

"That was an open goal, United," he drones on. "No wonder we're losing."

I'm only spared more insults because we almost go and let in another goal, and Coach strides off to shout at the defence.

"United?" repeats my marker, looking confused. "I thought you lot were called the Rovers?"

"We are," I sigh. Here it comes. I've had this kind of conversation many, many times before.

"So why did that man just say United?" he asks.

"Because he's my dad," I say.

"So?"

"And that's my name."

"What?"

"My name's United," I admit, feeling tempted to spell it out for him. I can tell he's not exactly overloaded with brain cells.

He nearly falls over laughing. "What kind of a stupid name is that?" he smirks.

"Mine," I say wearily, moving away to avoid further embarrassment.

I should be used to it by now I suppose, but it's even worse when I have to reveal my full name. Promise you won't laugh?

Really promise?

Well, okay, let's get it over with. It's United Newton Luck.

Oh, come on – you promised!

It's Dad's fault. He's totally mad about Manchester United, you see, and – sorry, I'll have to explain the Newton bit later, our team's on the attack again ...

Jag has just dribbled the ball over the halfway line, and he glances up to see where I am. Or more likely, knowing Jag, to check where the big guy is. I don't suppose Jag likes what he sees. Their big number five is heading straight for him like a laser, intent on revenge. Jag panics, hoofs the ball away and then doubles back as if to plug any gaps in midfield.

I control the dropping ball on my chest and find myself with only the keeper to beat. Before he can rush out to narrow the angle, I sweep the ball past him into the net.

GOAL!!!

I'm well into my usual dance routine before I realise I'm doing a solo jig. Nobody else has bothered to join in, and only now do I see why. The linesman is still waving his flag about and the referee is pointing for a free kick. I hadn't even heard the whistle!

"What's that for, ref?" I complain.

"Offside," he says, brushing aside all protests. "Get on with the game."

I can't believe it! Hands on hips, I glare across at the linesman. There's no way Rovers are going to win this match now. It's just not going to be our day.

My day doesn't get any better, either. I find myself being subbed just because I haven't scored for once.

I mean, I don't think that's really fair, do you?

I'm still sulking on the way home after the match, and Dad-Coach can sense I'm in a bad mood. Mind you, I might have made that pretty clear to everybody by kicking the water bucket up into the air as I left the pitch.

"I had to make some changes, United," he tells me. "And I can't afford to show any favouritism."

"I know that, Dad, but I am Rovers' top scorer this season," I mutter, dropping the 'Coach' stuff now we're in the car together.

Dad's not even listening. He's turned on the radio for the football commentary from Old Trafford. Manchester United are winning and he's happy again, our own defeat forgotten – and me as well possibly. Sometimes I wonder which United he really loves the most ...

Chapter 2 SUNDAY EVENING

"Pot! Here, boy!"

As usual, Pot does the opposite to what I tell him. The daft dog disappears round the corner and into the school playground.

"Pot!" I'm wasting my breath. He's got the scent of something and he's away, following his nose. I wish I hadn't let him off the lead now. He's always running off and I end up running after him, which is probably why I'm so fit, going for all these 'dog jogs' as Dad calls them.

It's no use calling out Pot's name. He has totally vanished. I sigh and squat down by the caretaker's hut to wait for my daft dog to reappear.

Caretaker – that's a joke. Old Grumpy doesn't take care of anything. He uses the hut to dump all sorts of broken things that he can't be bothered to mend.

Anyway, I was going to tell you about the rest of my name, wasn't I? Well, the 'Newton' bit refers to Manchester United's original name – Newton Heath. I think Dad only left out the 'Heath' bit so I'd be saddled with the initials U.N. for the rest of my life.

U.N. Luck. I mean, how UN-Luck-y can you get? It's definitely an UNgood name!

Hold on, I can hear something.

I peer round the hut, but what I see doesn't have whiskers, a dirty coat and a bushy tail. Well, no bushy tail, anyway.

It's Old Grumpy.

I'm afraid the caretaker and I don't exactly get on very well, but then again, Old Grumpy doesn't seem to get on well with anybody, not even the teachers. Mum's one of them, so I should know.

According to Mum, Old Grumpy thinks school would be a much better place without all the kids around causing him extra work.

He goes berserk at us when we play footie and tramp loads of mud into the cloakroom afterwards. Then he moans at Mum about all the mess, because she runs the school football and netball teams. He even grumbles about having to polish the cups that we win.

I'm surprised he's here at this time of the evening, but it's probably because of the break-ins. Our school's been broken into twice this year, so maybe he's checking that everywhere is locked up. Perhaps he does care after all? Then again, I doubt it.

The trouble with thieves is that they steal all the decent stuff like computers and TVs, and never touch the maths books and worksheets. Last time they even pinched the burglar alarms!

Pot chooses the wrong time to wander into view, snuffling around the bushes near the hut. Old Grumpy spots the dog and starts shouting and waving his arms to shoo him away.

Bad idea. That never works with Pot. He just thinks you want to play. He yelps with excitement, jumping up at the caretaker and easily dodging his wild kicks.

Old Grumpy looks like he's trying to do some strange, jerky dance, and it's hard for me not to laugh out loud. He ends up losing his balance and falls backwards into a big, prickly hedge.

Old Grumpy's not happy!

He finally pulls himself out of the hedge and gives up with the dog. I wait till he limps off, and then nip out from my hiding place to grab hold of Pot's collar.

It's only as we're about to make our escape that I notice our classroom window is wide open. "Typical!" I mutter. "I bet you made him miss that, Pot."

Torn between a sense of duty to close the window, and an even stronger sense of fear that Old Grumpy might return and see me with Pot, common sense wins out.

I leave.

Halfway home, feeling guilty, I change my mind and drag Pot back to the school. I must be mad, taking such a risk, but that's just me you see – UNsane.

That's when I see a leg disappearing through the window. The burglars must be back again!

It's a good job I have a mobile phone with

me. Mum insists I take it with me when I'm out with the dog. Emergency use only, she says – like if Pot gets lost. Well, this is an emergency, so I call the police and then hang about – at a safe distance – to see what happens when they arrive.

I get a big surprise when I finally find out who the leg belongs to, but I'll tell you about that later ...

CHAPTER 3 MONDAY MORNING

"Is this your drawer, Newton?"

I stare at the teacher. We both know it's a silly question. I mean, how many others have got 'United' written on them?

Not that Sir can ever bring himself to call me by that name. He hates football. Mind you, Sir's own name takes some beating. It's Mr Mister – so you can see why he prefers to be called Sir!

I can guess what's coming – and it isn't a prize for the best-kept drawer of the year.

"Well, it's a mess, as usual," he sneers. "No wonder it always takes you so long to find anything. Come and tidy it up."

Tidy it up, he says. That's a joke. I mean, there's so much stuff we're expected to have at school that I'd need a team of mules to carry it all here every day.

I scrape my chair across the floor and

start to weave a path through the maze of tables, chairs, bodies and bags that litter the classroom. I'm only about halfway there when I crash to the floor, bringing down a couple of shelves of books that failed to support my fall.

For a split second, I think that big ugly football hooligan has got me again ... I'm not far wrong. It's a pretty good description of Zoe too. She's the frizzy-haired monster with the outstretched leg.

"Oh, poor little Lucky took a tumble," cries Zoe, above all the whoops and cackles.

"Penalty!" claims one of her gang of mates sitting nearby.

"He dived!" shrieks another, as I struggle back onto my feet.

Sir isn't amused. "Be quiet, all of you, and get on with your work," he snaps before glaring at me. "I wouldn't be a bit surprised if you did that on purpose, Newton, just to raise a cheap laugh. You can now add sorting out that bookcase to your list of jobs after school – and I want all the authors in alphabetical order," he insists, ignoring the way I'm rubbing my knee in pain. "And don't forget about the gerbils."

As if I could. I've been looking forward all weekend to cleaning out their cage. I've hardly been able to sleep with excitement.

And if you believe that, you'll believe anything!

The truth is, most of this is Jag's fault. If Jag hadn't made me laugh in Friday assembly, then we wouldn't have been kept in at lunchtime, the gerbils wouldn't have escaped – and Sir wouldn't have been arrested! Let me explain ...

I can't remember now just what Jag said that was so funny, but Sir saw us laughing and he made us stand up in front of everyone.

"Jagdish! Newton! You will both be staying in at lunchtime to think about your behaviour."

Well that'll be a boring lunch hour, I thought. As it was, it turned out to be very UNboring!

So, there we were, in the classroom at lunchtime, and that's when Jag started it all. Okay, I admit it was my wild shot that smashed open the gerbil cage, but it was Jag's idea to have a kickabout with a tennis ball in the first place. We managed to recapture one of the gerbils before Sir came in, but the other vanished.

Gerbil on the loose!

Jag and I weren't going to risk another boring lunchtime by telling anyone what had happened and then getting into trouble again, so we both kept very quiet about the missing gerbil.

That brings me on to the mystery burglar. According to Mum, Sir came back to school that evening to collect some books for marking, then realised he'd forgotten his keys. He was about to go home when he saw the open window. That's when I saw the leg, and thought it belonged to a burglar! Mind you, Sir would've been long gone before the police arrived if he hadn't then seen Gerry the Gerbil.

The police found Sir crawling along the corridor on his hands and knees. For some strange reason, they wouldn't believe his story that he was just trying to catch a gerbil!

The thing is, the school suffered more vandalism yesterday, so no wonder Sir had some explaining to do. The trophy cabinet was smashed and all our sports cups have been stolen.

And Gerry's still on the run!

Chapter 4 **MONDAY AFTERNOON**

"What are you doing, Nitty?"

I don't need to turn round. Sir isn't the only one who asks me stupid questions.

"Can I play, Nitty?"

And at least Sir doesn't call me Nitty. This was my pesky kid sister's version of 'United' when she was even younger. Unfortunately, it's kind of stuck.

"No," I tell her. "I'm waiting for Jag."

I continue to kick a football against the school wall, hoping that Ollie will get bored and go away. No chance.

"Where is he?" she asks, keeping up her habit of talking in questions.

"Still having his dinner," I mutter, flicking the football up into the air and counting how many headers I can do before I lose control of the ball.

I only manage three.

"Get out of my way, Ollie!" I moan, putting the blame on her.

"Are you coming to watch our netball game after school, Nitty?"

"I'm busy."

"Doing what?"

I sigh, hoping that Jag will hurry up and rescue me.

"Sir's keeping me in again. I've got things to do."

"Like finding that poor little gerbil?" she asks.

"Yeah, maybe."

"Bet it's dead by now," she says, making it quite clear she thinks I'm guilty of murder. "Starved to death."

"Starved!" I exclaim. "There's so much food left lying about our classroom, the greedy thing's probably doubled in size."

Jag appears by my side. "Hope so," he grins. "It would make it easier to find."

I pull a face at him.

"It's about time you turned up," I mutter. "C'mon, let's go."

"Where to?"

"Anywhere that's not here," I say, glancing towards my sister, and Jag gets the message.

So does Ollie. "I've got netball practice soon, anyway, so there," she calls after us as we make for the playing field. "I'm in the team."

27

"Your sister's in the school team?" Jag says in amazement.

"Nah, it's only a game for the young kids before the main match starts."

"Is she any good?"

I check round to make sure Ollie isn't tagging along behind, listening.

"Yeah, she's okay. She'll be even better when she grows a bit. She catches the ball well – for a girl. It runs in the family."

"What does?"

"Sporting talent," I boast.

He chuckles. "Same with crazy names."

I give him one of my stares, but Jag's right of course. Ollie suffers almost as much as me.

Ollie was christened Olivia Wednesday Luck, so she has O.W.L. as her initials. Sheffield Wednesday are Mum's favourite football team, you see, and they're known as the Owls.

Jag and I knock the ball about between us. When one of my passes goes astray, Jag slumps down onto the grass with a grunt.

"I'm too full from dinner," he moans. "You fetch it, Lucky."

"Why me?"

"It's your ball."

It's also too late. Somebody else has already picked it up – Zoe.

She holds the ball out as if offering it back to me. I sigh and wander towards her, knowing there's no chance she will actually give it back.

"I'll toss you for it, little Lucky," she says, taking a coin from the pocket of her skirt. "Heads, I win – Tails, you lose. Okay?"

I nod. Sounds about right. I can't win either way.

She flips the coin in the air and I can't help but look how it lands. I mean, you never know. One of these days ...

"Tails!" she whoops. "Oh, what a pity, little Lucky! You've lost."

Surprise, surprise.

I make a grab for the ball, but it's gone.

Zoe has flicked it to one of her mates, who quickly passes it on to another. I find myself in the middle of a cackling triangle of girls.

"C'mon, little Lucky!" Zoe cries. "You're not even trying."

What's the point? I mean, they're all in the 'A' team at netball. I shrug and turn away and they run off, laughing, towards the netball court to watch the younger girls play instead.

"Why don't you go and tell Mother Hen?" says Jag.

"That's my mother you're talking about," I remind him with a stare.

Jag tends to forget sometimes and uses Mum's school nickname in front of me. It comes from the way Mum writes her name on forms – C. Luck.

"Oh, yeah, right," he grins.

"A big help that'd be, anyway," I mutter. "It'd only make them do stupid things like that even more."

I decide to go and find my ball, but there's no sign of Zoe's lot – or my ball.

I can see where it's been, though. I follow a trail of muddy marks that lead me into the school and along the corridor towards our classroom.

There are even patches of mud on the walls and ceiling. "Old Grumpy will have a fit when he sees all this mess," I murmur, somehow sensing that I'll be the one who gets the blame.

I'm right too. I find the ball – well, the round thing covered in mud, that is – plonked on my chair, with dirty streaks right across the table top.

I pick the ball up, very carefully, just as I hear somebody come into the room. I turn, expecting to see Zoe or even Sir, but it's Old Grumpy himself.

This is definitely an UNgood moment. I'm caught brown-handed.

I spend the first part of the afternoon mopping the floors and wiping the walls – watched by Old Grumpy – then Sir gives me a pile of worksheets to do while everyone else is painting and making models.

I mean, I don't think that's really fair, do you?

"Ah, poor little Lucky!" coos Zoe when she comes by, flicking paint off her brush onto my book.

Sir even stays in the room after school, marking, just to make sure I don't waste time watching the netball match through the window. Instead, I waste time clearing away all the stuff from the art and craft session, and even looking for Gerry again.

I do manage to find some sign of where he's been – and so I have to clean that mess up too.

By the time I'm allowed to leave, the netball has finished. Ollie has scored a goal – or whatever they call it in netball when the ball goes through the hoop. She grabs me by the arm and natters on for ages about her moment of glory.

I'm rescued by Zoe, of all people, who tells Ollie to buzz off.

"Sorry about you having to clean up all that mud," Zoe says in a low voice, making sure that no one else can hear. "Some people would've blabbed."

"I'm not like that."

"I know – but thanks, anyhow."

"That's okay."

"You're okay – really," she smiles. "But don't tell anyone I said that, little Lucky!"

CHAPTER 5 MONDAY EVENING

Yep, here I am again – back at school. I seem to be spending most of my life at this place these days.

Dad-Coach hires the school hall for Rovers' indoor training sessions on Monday evenings. He likes to put the squad through what he calls a 'good work-out'. We kids call it torture.

I'm only able to speak now without panting because we've got a bit of a break while Coach sticks one of our defenders back together again. The clumsy kid just half-knocked himself out after running into a wall during a relay race. His brakes must have failed!

"Wake up, United!"

Coach's shout stirs me back into action. I hadn't realised the races had started again and I tear off across the hall well behind the other runners.

It's an obstacle course, and the only reason I catch Jag so quickly is because he's got himself tangled up, crawling beneath one of the goal nets. Being small, I slither under it more easily than most, then zigzag through a row of cones as if dribbling past a group of dummy defenders.

My undoing is a wet patch on the floor, where I try to cut a corner and skid out of control.

It's lucky that I have a soft landing. It's UNlucky that it's on top of the poor kid who was already wounded and sitting at the side. At least it gives me a chance to pretend I'm hurt too, and miss the rest of the torture.

I think I'll wait till the five-a-side games start before I declare myself fit enough to rejoin the action. Mum turns up at this point with Ollie. They've left Pot tied up in the playground while they come indoors.

"I've just got a few things I need to sort out in my classroom," she explains to me. "Go with Olivia, will you, and give Pot a run round the field."

"But Mum, I can't. I'm seriously injured," I tell her.

"Where?" she asks.

"Everywhere," I moan.

Mum looks at me and raises an eyebrow. The trouble is, Mum always seems to know when I'm not telling the truth. I bet yours does too, when you're trying to get away with something. I mean, how do they know? It's UNcanny!

"Nonsense," says Mum. "A bit of exercise will do you good."

Huh! A bit of exercise is exactly what I'm trying to avoid! I get slowly to my feet, groaning and grumbling, but Mum's not impressed. She's seen my acting many times before.

"C'mon, Ollie," I mutter. "Let's go."

Still, if it's a choice between risking life and limb on Dad's obstacle course, or taking Pot for a walk, I think I know which I'd rather do. There's no way, though, that I'm going to risk letting Pot have a run. If he's let off the lead, he'll just disappear into the dark.

But we're too late. When we get outside, there's no sign of Pot.

"Where is he?" wails Ollie.

"Who tied him up?" I sigh, knowing what the answer's going to be.

"Me," she confesses in a pathetic little voice.

We find him sooner than expected.

He's making a right racket by the door of the old hut. Pot's so busy barking, I'm able to grab his trailing lead and try to pull him away. He won't budge. He can be very stubborn at times.

"Perhaps he's trying to tell us something," says Ollie.

Sigh – I think she's been watching too many Lassie films.

"The only thing he's trying to tell us," I grunt, yanking on the lead in vain, "is that he doesn't want to go for walkies."

Ollie isn't listening. She lifts the latch of the hut door and, to my surprise, it swings open. Old Grumpy normally keeps it padlocked, so he must still be around somewhere.

"What are you doing, Ollie?" I whisper. "Have you gone mad? If Old Grumpy catches us here he'll –"

Ollie suddenly dives forward into the hut.

"I've got him!" she squeals and comes out holding Gerry the Gerbil up high in triumph.

"Pot must have smelt him."

It's definitely our Gerry. The end of his tail is missing. It came off last term and we never did find out how. Perhaps Zoe tossed a coin and he lost!

"Fancy a chip, little Lucky?"

I whirl round and find Zoe herself right behind me.

"Where did you come from?"

"The chippie," she grins, holding out the bag. "Have a couple, if you like."

I shake my head. "I can't. I'm training."

"Get him to sit, then, will you?" she demands, having to keep the bag away from Pot's quivering nose. He's lost all interest in the gerbil now.

"I mean football training, not dog training."

"What, with Rubbish Rovers?"

I change the subject, but can't help noticing that Zoe hasn't offered Ollie or even Gerry a chip, never mind Pot.

"You're allowed out after dark on your own, are you?"

"It's not too dark yet," Zoe says with a shrug. "I was just on my way home when I heard all this barking, so I came to see what was happening."

"I found Gerry in the hut," Ollie boasts.

"It's about time that thing turned up," Zoe chuckles, stuffing her mouth with chips. "What else is in there?"

"I haven't looked," I admit.

"Well, let's take a peek, then, little Lucky."

Sometimes it pays to be nosy. We peer inside the hut and there, on the floor, is a sackful of trophies.

"The cups!" I cry.

"Oi! Get out of my hut!"

I turn to see the caretaker striding towards us. Pot starts barking again, but Old Grumpy's in no mood to play. I've never seen him look so mad – and that's saying something.

"What are you lot doing here?" he yells.

"Never mind us," I cry, holding the sack up in the air. "What are these doing here?"

"I'm cleaning them."

"No, you're not," Zoe shouts. "You've stolen them!"

"So what?" he snorts. "Now I'll never have to clean those things again. I know a chap on the market who'll give me a few quid for 'em."

Suddenly it all makes sense. I bet this chap has had our computers and other valuable stuff too.

"You're a thief!" I accuse him. "It's been you all along."

Old Grumpy sniggers. "Prove it!"

"We'll tell the police," cries Ollie defiantly.

"Who'll believe little kids like you?"

"I will," says a voice.

49

It's Mum. She must have heard our loud voices and the barking and come out to see what's happening. For once, I'm glad that she always seems to know what's going on!

"I think you have some explaining to do," she tells Old Grumpy. "I'm shocked that you would do such a thing. Come with me back inside – now! And bring all those cups too."

You should see Old Grumpy's face. It's a picture of misery as he takes the sack from me and trails after Mum into the school.

Somehow, I don't think he's going to be our caretaker very much longer. In fact, I bet he'll soon be getting another kind of a sack!

"Come on!" says Zoe, still guzzling her chips. "Let's follow them. I want to see what's going to happen."

Plenty happens – and all inside the next few seconds ...

"Stop him!" I hear Mum scream as we enter the building. "Don't let him escape!"

And she doesn't mean Gerry either.

51

We rush into the noisy hall, to see Old Grumpy dashing through all the obstacles that litter the floor …

… a stray ball hits Zoe and bursts her bag of chips, sharing them at last with Pot and Ollie who manage to catch a few before they drop …

… then Old Grumpy trips over some of the cones and scatters the cups across the mats …

… Jag moves in and throws the netting over him …

... Dad gets ready to grab the caretaker, but he's not needed ...

... because I've already got him!

I used the first thing that came to hand – or rather, to foot. I don't really know why I lashed out at the ball as it bounced off Zoe, but I've never struck such a sweet volley.

It sped like a bullet towards its target – Old Grumpy. He was just struggling up onto his knees when the ball smacked him right on the back of the head and laid him out flat.

What a goal!

55

"Best shot I've ever seen!" laughs Dad, while Old Grumpy is being led away by the police. "We'll have another one like that next Sunday, please, United."